Intuition

Intuition

The Science of Self

Murray Ash

ISBN: 979-8-218-47361-7

To listen beyond thoughts and see beneath beliefs.

To seek understanding.

To embrace the wisdom of experience and express our authentic Self.

This is intuition's desire.

I wrote this book for those embracing the path of Self-mastery. It's created in loving memory of my brother Finlay and with gratitude to my mother, Sandie; without you, none of this would have been possible. To Lynn Traub, my devoted guide and tutor, your dedication taught me unconditional love. I'm grateful to my teachers, Dr. Gabor Maté and Sat Dharam Kaur N.D., for showing me how to transmute my lessons into teachings.

◣ Introduction

Each section of this book serves as a faithful compass on your journey to finding purpose. Self-understanding is an inquiry revealing the sublimity of who you've always been. You'll go beyond the learned aspects of your personality and experience the unveiled Self. 'Self' refers to your essence — the authentic 'you' beneath your conditioned attachments and personas. This exploration is not merely about change but reconnection with yourself, your aspirations, and your authenticity; in essence, it's the true you.

Throughout this book, you'll be asked to recall recent situations. Use any situational experience you want to resolve, understand or overcome. If you're processing something specific, such as a breakup or personal loss, using the same example for each entry may benefit you. However, if you are working with a particular pattern, behaviour, or addiction that continues to affect your life negatively, utilising separate events may serve you well. Each section should take no more than thirty minutes to complete.

Entries consist of contextual introductions followed by free writing prompts. Free writing is a spontaneous and unrestricted creative technique that allows your thoughts to flow onto paper without worrying about grammar, structure, or coherence. To accomplish this, write continuously using the exercise prompts for guidance, resisting the urge to edit or analyse your work. The goal is to bypass your inner critic and conscious mind to uncover ideas that may not surface in reflective thought alone. This technique requires you to write until you think about what to say next, then immediately move on to the following prompt.

Day 1: Contemplation

Today serves as the foundation for your introspective journey. Your goal is to articulate a comprehensive description of yourself. Draw inspiration from the meaningful life experiences that shaped who you are as you describe your personality.

◖ Phase 1 Self-Reflection (Days 1-6)

Day 1 - Write: Recognise the patterns, habits, and nuances intricately shaping your unique identity. How did they influence your beliefs and values? Reflect on pivotal experiences that shaped your character using the following prompts. If your life was a novel, and you were the main character, describe your qualities, strengths, and weaknesses. Consider childhood environments, family dynamics and their internal systems, specific memories, and significant relationships. How did these connections influence your values? Which routine behaviours or characteristics currently drain your energy? Examine a recent challenge – what habits supported you, and which presented obstacles?

_____

_____

_____

_____

_____

_____

_____

_____

_____

_____

_____

_____

_____

_____

_____

_____

_____

_____

_____

_____

Day 2: Initial Reflection

Read yesterday's entry. Highlight or underline the parts that stand out to you.
Bring awareness to how your body responds to your description of yourself.

◢ **Phase 1** Self-Reflection (Days 1-6)

Day 2 - Write: What kind of person did you read about in your portrayal? Which areas of life would that person seek assistance with? Is there anything you forgot to mention in your description? If so, how do you feel about that? Can you identify any obstacles keeping you from happiness? Do you recognise barriers preventing you from living a fulfilling, purpose-led life? Reflect on criticism from friends, family, or partners. Which of these observations remains poignant? Notice which details you attach to, regardless of whether you believe them to be true or false.

_____

_____

_____

_____

_____

_____

_____

_____

_____

_____

_____

_____

_____

_____

_____

_____

_____

_____

_____

_____

_____

Day 3: Feelings vs. Perceptions

Feelings are bodily experiences such as tingling, warmth, tension, or heaviness. They are always valid; however, we learn to allocate meaning to our feelings during childhood, forming beliefs and perceptions about ourselves. We do this to protect ourselves from perceived threats, such as a lack of safety or pain. Although temporarily helping us make sense of what's happening around us, these perceptions, if left unattended, persist as inauthentic behaviours later in life.

Perceptions are adaptations to our true Self that we create to protect us from experiencing the painful truth of a situation. One such example could be the realisation that our caregivers are emotionally unavailable or disconnected, meaning they are unable to hold our pain. If we were taught how to hold pain, we wouldn't have trauma. Examples of perceptions are 'they abandoned me', 'they rejected me', 'they invalidated me', or 'I am alone'. Notice how these aren't feelings. One can perceive they are alone, yet there is no physiological sensation of loneliness.

Perceptions are limiting as they shape our reality, our experience of others and our worldview. In these beliefs, we relinquish our strength, autonomy, happiness, and, most importantly, our authenticity. In adulthood, we believe these adaptations are who we truly are. Many of us go through our entire lives believing we're someone we're not. The cost of suffering a life framed by beliefs is far greater than the brief, sharp awakening brought on by experiencing truth, for in truth lies growth.

◀▶ **Phase 1** Self-Reflection (Days 1-6)

Day 3 - Write: Explore a recent emotionally triggering experience. Distinguish between the raw feeling (e.g. throat constriction) and the perceptions your mind attached to it (e.g. I'm not lovable). It's important not to make yourself right or wrong but to explore why this perception was present. What was going on for you at that moment? What did the presence of the perception do for you? What did it keep you safe from feeling or experiencing at that moment? Secondly, consider a recent positive experience. Distinguish between genuine feelings of joy or contentment and any perceptions that might arise to keep you safe from feeling too much (e.g. a fear that it won't last, being unworthy or questioning why this is happening to you). Where did your feelings and perceptions clash? How did your feelings differ from the beliefs you assigned to the situation?

_____

_____

_____

_____

_____

_____

_____

_____

_____

_____

_____

_____

_____

_____

_____

_____

_____

Day 4: Identifying Behaviour Patterns

Psychologist Richard C Schwartz's work on Inner Family Systems, or 'IFS', speaks of different aspects or 'parts' of our Self. Our essence, or the part of us beneath the adaptations we formed to protect us from vulnerability (meaning the capacity to be wounded), is peaceful, joyful, and connected. Yet, this true 'Self' is often the most challenging version of us to accept. It's commonly the antithesis of our perceptions about who we are or who we've understood ourselves to be. Without Self-acceptance, we cannot be compassionate, internally calm, or respond responsibly in our communication. Many of our behaviours stem from these parts. One part of us wants to control and protect our wounded pieces from being seen, arising, or losing their power. This part often has us victimising ourselves or carrying a sense of entitlement that we want to hide in our relationships. These parts are inner critics, and they have us seeking social approval through our appearance and financial or societal status. Another part is reactive. It shows up as physical illness and pain that subdues us or manifests as stress that triggers autoimmune disorders. It distracts us from our perceptions of shame, rejection, or fear. Although well-intentioned, these parts prevent us from growing, preoccupying us with illusions of safety.

It is within these vulnerable parts, the parts that feel they need protecting, that we find our roles. Our roles are the aspects of ourselves we shy away from to protect against the memories, pain, or shame of having them reappear in our present expression of the past. These are unwanted, inauthentic behaviours, such as neediness, anxiety, avoidance, and shame. Healing starts with intentionally confronting these parts that we've spent a lifetime avoiding. What resistance masks, persistence grasps, so perseverance will be a consistent topic during your work in this book. As we begin to confront and inquire into these beliefs and perceptions, many of these parts will shift from protective roles to welcoming and connective qualities. Focus on these internal parts of yourself today.

◗ **Phase 1** Self-Reflection (Days 1-6)

Day 4 - Write: Use a recent situation to draw parallels between the actions of these parts and your inward experience, both during the event and after. Articulate the interactions and conflicts between these internal parts. What did each part want? What aspect of yourself did one part want to prevent being seen or arising? Did you feel entitled to something you didn't get? What did it have you pursue for gratification? What did these parts make the event mean about you? Did a part arise that had you shut down or experience stress? What could they have been trying to keep you safe from? What can you thank them for so they can drop their roles and promote a newfound life of connection through authentic expression?

_____

_____

_____

_____

_____

_____

_____

_____

_____

_____

_____

_____

_____

_____

_____

_____

_____

_____

Day 5: The Emotional Body

Emotions are bodily reactions to our mind, such as fear, joy, and stress. They differ from feelings, which are pre-cognitive sensations, meaning they occur before our mind forms thoughts around them. Emotions are attempts to understand our present feelings. For many, our initial trauma points back to the first moment our emotions weren't met with a safe relational container, meaning our primary caregivers were unable to tolerate our emotions and withdrew connection. At this moment, we experienced a disconnection from the only love we understood. The perception we make about ourselves whilst experiencing these emotions is the trauma, not what happened. Ultimate suffering hides in the emotions we can't handle. Misery is resisting the emotions we don't think we can hold.

◖▸ **Phase 1** Self-Reflection (Days 1-6)

Day 5 - Write: Write about a time you had to suppress your emotions. Were you comfortable sharing this pain with your caregivers? How did they respond? Were they available to hold space for you in this? What did you have to adjust in your Self-expression to reconnect with them? Who did you have to become to be deemed acceptable by them? What did you make this adaptation mean about who you are? Where did you have to sacrifice your authentic emotional expression to reattach for safety? Where were you acting out to ensure the security of the relationship wasn't threatened by sharing your genuine emotional experience?

_____

_____

_____

_____

_____

_____

_____

_____

_____

_____

_____

_____

_____

_____

_____

_____

_____

Day 6: Comprehending the Functionality of Behaviours

To understand what we do, we must first gain insight into the functionality of our behaviours. We need to ask what's right about a problematic behaviour by identifying its purpose instead of judging what's wrong with it. After all, every addiction or addictive behaviour fulfils some need. Becoming conscious of the costs of behaviours outweighing the payoffs allows us to begin making changes. Fill in the following cost and payoff sheet to explore and understand existing patterns or addictions.

Day 6 - Cost and Payoff Sheet: Write down the behaviour you'll be working with as a title. In the costs category, identify undesirable or unwanted consequences, drawbacks, or challenges linked to the behaviour or addiction. Examples could be social alienation, financial burden, health risks or energetic depletion. These can be short-term or long-term implications on your physical, mental or emotional well-being, impacts on relationships, work performance or anything detrimental to your personal fulfilment and purposeful alignment.

Outline the benefits or rewards gained from this behaviour in the payoffs section. Explore how the behaviour might fulfil specific needs or desires. Examples could be providing a sense of calmness, distraction from pain, social connection, straightforward connectivity to pleasure, or simply disconnecting from undesirable and taxing tasks.

Title: _____

Cost	Payoff

Cost	Payoff

Day 7: The Somatic Experience

Today, we begin integrating the body connection, encouraging a focused awareness of the physiological response to emotional experiences. Peter Levine, PhD, developed Somatic Experiencing, a naturalistic, neurobiological approach to healing trauma. As we previously explored in the feelings section, somatic experiences relate to the body and are distinct from the mind. They are both pre-cognitive and pre-verbal and are telltale signs that something from our past is affecting our present reality experience. Exploring these responses is invaluable, as they allow us access to our repressed and blocked experiences through implicit memories, meaning those we cannot explicitly recall.

◀▶ Phase 2 Present Moment Awareness (Days 7-9)

Day 7 - Write: Explore your somatic experience by identifying your body's response to a recent situation. These sensations could be comfortable or uncomfortable, but don't allow yourself to give power to the meaning you gave; instead, write about the bodily experience itself. Take a moment to breathe and explore all areas of your body as you recall the event. What happened? If others were present, what did they say or do? What were your surroundings? How did your body react to this environment? Recognise what you feel in your torso and your shoulders. How do your palms feel? Notice what your legs want to do; are they grounded, or do they want to move? Pinpoint and specify the locations in your body where you experience these sensations. However minimal, write down every detail of your somatic experience around this situation.

Day 8: Triggers

Recount a recent challenging situation where you reacted to something someone said or did. This exercise encourages you to describe a factual account. It lays the groundwork for deeper exploration and interpretation of subsequent actions and reflections.

Day 8 - Write: Describe the details of the situation without subjective interpretation, focusing only on what factually transpired. Identify triggers within the exchange and specify the words and actions of the individuals involved, such as 'they said' and 'I said' statements. Notice where you want to add context or judgment or use feeling, emotion, or perception descriptors to justify or rationalise behaviours.

_____

_____

_____

_____

_____

_____

_____

_____

_____

_____

_____

_____

_____

_____

_____

_____

_____

_____

_____

_____

Day 9: Connecting with the Present Moment, Familiarity and the First Time

Using yesterday's recently recalled situation, re-immerse yourself in the present bodily experience. Utilise your somatic response to the memory. If you struggle with connecting to a sensation, firstly focus on the palms of your hands and notice what's there. Maybe there's heat or moisture, or they're clammy and tense. Continue following that awareness into each part of your body until you're conscious of the location of its response to this memory. Be aware of the habit pattern of your mind wanting to disconnect from the feeling, and ensure you don't allow it to become an emotion or perception.

Day 9 - Write: Is this a new feeling or something familiar? If it's familiar, how old is it? Use the feeling to revisit the first time you felt this sensation. How was your life at this time? What was happening in your family? Did you have friends? How did you feel at this age? What did you want or need that you weren't getting? Take these answers and form a statement for use in tomorrow's exercise, where we'll begin understanding the Self more clearly. A demonstrative statement could be: When my parents told me they were getting divorced, I felt a sudden heaviness in my chest. The emotions present were fear and anger, and I needed support that wasn't available.

_____

_____

_____

_____

_____

_____

_____

_____

_____

_____

_____

_____

_____

_____

_____

_____

_____

_____

Day 10: Exploring Childhood Experiences

This exercise will uncover early connections between emotions and experiences, shedding light on the origins of certain beliefs and behaviours. All living beings are flawed, but in childhood, we cannot comprehend that our primary caregivers are imperfect. That realisation would leave a child believing that they're entirely unsafe in the world. After all, not only do we perceive our parents as gods, but they are also our first experience of love when we are attuned and later heartbreak when we lose connection to them.

Day 10 - Write: Write out your final statement from day 9. What did you make it mean about yourself? Using yesterday's example, one could have made it mean they weren't worthy of loving support or that they must suppress their natural anger to be accepted. What personal explanation did you administer as a panacea for this wounded part? Explore your interpretations. Where did you attribute the fault to yourself in lieu of the capacity to perceive parental shortcomings? Reflect on the significance of this childhood experience. How has it materialised throughout your life? How is it currently affecting your decisions and patterns? Who would you be without this belief?

_____

_____

_____

_____

_____

_____

_____

_____

_____

_____

_____

_____

_____

_____

_____

_____

_____

_____

_____

Day 11: Navigating the Autonomic Nervous System

The autonomic nervous system is a network of nerves that regulate involuntary physiological processes, such as respiratory and heart rates. The work of Dr. Steven Porges, PhD, presents a fascinating way of understanding the neurophysiology of emotions, communication, and Self-regulation, meaning our perceptions of ourselves and the world. He calls this Polyvagal Theory. Poly, meaning 'many', and Vagal, referring to the Vagus nerve, denotes multiple autonomic response states. It theorises that our autonomic nervous system responds differently to situational events and perceived threats. We can learn to recognise our responses and behavioural patterns by identifying our autonomic nervous system states. The nervous system transports information via the vagus nerve to induce a fight-flight, fawn, or freeze response to soothe the body. It's imperative to experience what's happening in our physiological state to comprehend how and why we respond the way we do. Brain circuits of traumatised people get confused and can identify safety or a threat where there is none. The three states are named Sympathetic, Ventral, and Dorsal.

1. The Sympathetic physiological state supports mobilisation. It's commonly known as the fight or flight response to external stimuli. It's associated with argumentative, defensive behaviour, particularly verbal or physical. However, it brings us into co-regulation when supported by play, such as movement and smiling at one another. Our movement progresses to aggressive behaviour without these welcoming actions.

2. Ventral is a physiological state of calmness that supports our ability to engage with one another in a functionally co-regulated, relaxed state of homeostasis. In the Ventral state, we subconsciously sense safety (neuroception) to connect through present, authentic, secure attachment.

3. Dorsal is the most evolutionary primitive part of our nervous system. It's the physiological state associated with the freeze response, which looks like passively being in a situation without engaging. For the most part, this can be thought of as being unable to move, such as struggling to get out of bed. In the dorsal state, everything seems complicated, and the world appears as an unwelcoming, exhaustive place. It's a defensive response of shutting down when overwhelmed. However, if we can maintain social engagement, the immobilisation response can transmute into moments of intimacy, where we're comfortable in the proximity of others.

Day 11 - Write: Deb Dana, LCSW, translated Polyvagal Theory into a simple exercise to show how the nervous system works. Reflect on experiences when you entered these states, recognising the differences in your perceptions. Fill in the following table for each response. Describe how the world seems in this state and how you perceive yourself.

Sympathetic State	Neuroception of danger with the impulse to act. Fight/Flight. Insecure attachment — survival of the individual or group.
World Appearance: Describe how the world seems to you when in a sympathetic state, e.g. hostile.	
Self-Perception: How do you perceive yourself in this state, e.g. anxious?	

Ventral State

Neuroception of safety to connect.
Presence. Secure attachment.

World Appearance:
Explore how the world
appears when in a ventral
state, e.g. settled or safe.

Self-Perception:
How do you feel about
yourself in this state, e.g.
grounded?

Dorsal State

Neuroception of threat with immobilisation or paralysis. Freeze. Insecure attachment — survival of the individual.

World Appearance:
How does the world appear when in a dorsal state, e.g. impossible?

Self-Perception:
How are you in this state, e.g. helpless?

Day 12: Navigating Support

In previous entries, you reflected on an earlier time in life, recalling the emotions felt at a specific age and recognised the associated meanings you attributed to various events.

Day 12 - Write: Revisit the same experience. Who did you speak to about your feelings at that time? If you confided in someone, explain the reasons behind choosing them. Who was it? Did their understanding, listening ability, empathic presence, or other qualities draw you to them? If you didn't have someone to talk to, why do you believe that was? Was it a lack of trust, presence, safety, or a fear of judgment? If you couldn't go to your primary caregivers, why not?

Craft a final statement after this exercise that looks something like this. When I was six, I was bullied at school. The feeling was a pulsing sensation in my solar plexus. My legs wanted to run, and emotionally, I felt stressed. At that time, I made it mean I was weak, and I didn't talk to my father because he would have said I needed to toughen up.

_____

_____

_____

_____

_____

_____

_____

_____

_____

_____

_____

_____

_____

_____

Day 13: Compassionate Validation

Compassion comes from the understanding that all unwanted behaviours serve a protective purpose. Empathise with your inner child's experience, recognising their quest for safety.

Day 13 - Write: Revisit yesterday's event. Picture a child you know or a child in general at that age. Envision how the child might feel in a similar situation. How could they re-establish the connection with safety lost at that time? What would they have to do? What might they make doing that mean about themselves? How might they adapt their personality or create their persona following that experience? Who might they become? What attachments would they have to form to survive a repeated experience?

_____

_____

_____

_____

_____

_____

_____

_____

_____

_____

_____

_____

_____

_____

_____

_____

_____

_____

Day 14: Reparenting the Inner Child

Yesterday, you envisioned a child going through a similar experience to your own. Today, we will investigate understanding and resolution.

◀▶ Phase 3 Past-Present Relationship (Days 10-15)

Day 14 - Write: Who would you want them to talk to if you were the child's parent from day 12? Would it be you? If so, why? If not you, why not? Explore the reasons behind this decision. Could these reasons reflect your own? Using your work so far in understanding perceptions, what alternative reasons could there be to understand your inner child's experience? Had you been able to talk to your caregivers, who might you be now?

_____

_____

_____

_____

_____

_____

_____

_____

_____

_____

_____

_____

_____

_____

_____

_____

_____

_____

_____

_____

_____

Day 15: Exploring Core Beliefs

Core beliefs lie beneath our conscious understanding of ourselves. Less
powerful, easier-to-deal-with beliefs usually conceal them from our
recognition. An example could be the belief that I need to be quieter to be
accepted by my partner. Meanwhile, the core belief beneath that contains a
far larger fear-invoking childhood sentiment that if I'm myself, my caregivers
will abandon me.

◀▶ Phase 3 Past-Present Relationship (Days 10-15)

Day 15 - Write: Consider a recent event where you felt hurt or disconnected from your true Self. What belief was present? Notice how it serves as an anchor, keeping you shackled to unwanted perceptions, behaviours, and addictions. Write five sentences structured as follows. When... happened at/aged..., I believed... and my core belief was... For example, when I got my bad school results at sixteen, I believed I was stupid. My core belief was that I was not enough because I made my perception that I was stupid mean I would never be accepted or loved.

_____

_____

_____

_____

_____

_____

_____

_____

_____

_____

_____

_____

_____

_____

_____

_____

_____

_____

_____

Day 16: Coping Mechanisms and Addictions

Although liberating, the truth is often painful. Coping mechanisms are functional behaviours with the sole job of protecting us from feeling this pain. Coping mechanisms are forms of addictive behaviour. An addiction can be defined as any pattern of behaviour in which we crave temporary relief or pleasure regardless of negative long-term consequences. It's addictive because we can't give it up despite these negative impacts. As we use these mechanisms to hide from pain, and as Dr. Gabor Maté states, it's beneficial to ask not why the addiction or behaviour, but why the pain? Explore your coping mechanisms, such as substance use, harmful activities, maladaptive emotional reactions, physical self-harm, isolation or negative thought processes. Recognise their role in responding to and supporting underlying beliefs to keep you from encountering painful yet liberating truths. When we can identify the pain, we can learn to hold it instead of using coping mechanisms to hide from it. The purpose of self-work and therapy is to learn to hold our pain. Remember, our natural reaction to pain is to change something to get rid of it, but healing means observing our pain and detaching from the story we assign to it. As a side note, Vipassana, meaning to see things as they are, is a meditation technique designed specifically for this and is highly recommended.

◢◤ Phase 4 Coping and Self-Compassion (Days 16-18)

Day 16 - Write: Identify your coping mechanisms. For example, some people have the core belief, 'I'm alone in the world', and they develop a habitual behaviour of pushing partners away so they never have to feel the pain of being left alone. Which behavioural patterns continually reappear in your life? Why do they persist? What behavioural means of coping do you most commonly utilise? What need or purpose do they serve in light of understanding your core beliefs? What are their negative or costly, long-term implications? What truth are they keeping you from accepting? What temporary pain exists in that acceptance? Who would you be if you accepted that truth?

_____

_____

_____

_____

_____

_____

_____

_____

_____

_____

_____

_____

_____

_____

_____

_____

_____

_____

Day 17: Embracing Compassion for our Behaviours

Yesterday, we explored our current behaviours as adaptations of childhood coping mechanisms. It's important to recognise that seeking comfort, connection, or safety is intrinsic to the human experience. However, employing adaptive childhood strategies in adulthood ultimately prevents authentic connection and Self-mastery as we react instead of responding. Recognising the utility of our behaviour allows us to shift from judgment to appreciation for its intention to keep us safe. With this insight, we can make informed choices based on truth to maintain or change our way of being.

Day 17 - Write: Does this behaviour fulfil an ordinary human need? Is there another way you could meet your requirements? Why are these childhood behaviours still present now? Consider what they provide. Do they aim to comfort, offer control, or relieve stress? What do they want to protect you from? How could you thank them for their protection and let them know they're no longer needed? If you changed these behaviours, what self-imposed labels could you release? What beliefs could you let go of? Who would you be without them? How would the world appear in the absence of these behaviours?

_____

_____

_____

_____

_____

_____

_____

_____

_____

_____

_____

_____

_____

_____

_____

_____

_____

_____

_____

_____

Day 18: Challenging Current Beliefs

Phases 1-4 prompted cognitive flexibility as you challenged limiting beliefs through behavioural understanding. You've begun to accept your past behaviours as protective strategies and identified the benefits and functionalities of your core beliefs. With this clarity of understanding, we will complete phase 4 by reframing the limitations of past events in preparation for entering phase 5, embracing the world of change.

◢◤ Phase 4 Coping and Self-Compassion (Days 16-18)

Day 18 - Write: Explore a recent, significant event when someone said or did something that upset you. Write about the narrative you attached to the situation, separating the factual events from the story. What was said or done? Focus on your perceptive state and core beliefs. Which vagal state did your body enter? How would someone in that state perceive the world and themselves? What limitations could your perception have perpetuated? Explore possible alternate reasons for their actions and your interpretation of them. How might the situation be perceived from a different perspective or vagal state? How might the world appear if you didn't hold on to this belief? Describe how this shift could influence your perceptions of reality. Without these constraints, who would you be? How could this evolution direct you toward your path to purpose?

_____

_____

_____

_____

_____

_____

_____

_____

_____

_____

_____

_____

_____

_____

_____

_____

_____

Day 19: Embracing Personal Responsibility

Responsibility, or the ability to respond from our present, authentic, adult Self, means we're no longer re-acting from our childhood survival adaptations. Remember, within us all exists both the experience of a wounded child and the capacity to respond as a healed adult. It is up to us and our Self-awareness to decide which one we respond from. People will do what they do from either of these places; our strength comes from not allowing it to derail our present, healed Self and fall into the familiar adaptations of our inner wounded child. Imagine what would change if you could re-write your story to shift the focus from what someone said or did to acknowledging the power of owning and choosing your response.

◢◤ Phase 5 Welcoming Change (Days 19-21)

Day 19 - Write: Write about your accountability for your actions during a recent event. In your writing, utilise your understanding of Polyvagal Theory and the autonomic nervous system's perception of threat. Where could you be responsible for your situational interpretation and response? Which parts of you were triggered, hurt or protective in your reaction? How old are they? Reflect on the impact of your interpretations in your response. How do your perceptions, reactions, and actions contribute to your growth and interactions with others? How would this change if you were able to maintain responsibility more frequently?

_____

_____

_____

_____

_____

_____

_____

_____

_____

_____

_____

_____

_____

_____

_____

_____

_____

Day 20: A Taste of Potential

Now that we've practised reframing perceptions, we'll begin affirming
achievements. Savouring success is imperative to Self-discovery, as it allows us
to be compassionate to our past actions whilst encouraging further personal
development.

◢▏ **Phase 5** Welcoming Change (Days 19-21)

Day 20 - Write: What are your strengths? What talents and capabilities have you developed through your experiences? What obstacles have you overcome to get to where you are now? What have you already achieved in life that your child Self would admire? Which accomplishments are you proud of? Can you recognise the work you've done and are currently doing as a learning phase or a time for betterment and Self-mastery? Describe how. What would you say to yourself about your journey so far? How would you thank your younger Self for showing up and persevering through these challenging times?

Day 21: Attachments

Modern psychotherapy and psychology categorise personality adaptations into three main attachment styles: Secure, Anxious, and Avoidant. There is much literature on this subject, but to simplify attachment theory and styles for self-reflection, we will categorise each one as follows. Secure people are comfortable with intimacy and independence, anxious people fear abandonment and seek consistent external reassurance, and avoidant people feel uncomfortable with emotional intimacy and are generally distrusting.

◆ **Phase 5** Welcoming Change (Days 19-21)

Day 21 - Write: Which attachment style do you most identify with? How might your attachment style have influenced your behaviours and relationships? Have you always functioned this way, or has it changed over time? If so, what memorable event altered your way of being? What was happening at that time? What kinds of attachment styles have you attracted in partners? How are these familiar to your upbringing and relationships with primary caregivers?

_____

_____

_____

_____

_____

_____

_____

_____

_____

_____

_____

_____

_____

_____

_____

_____

_____

"Your conflicts, all the difficult things, the problematic situations in your life are not chance or haphazard. They are actually yours. They are specifically yours, designed specifically for you by a part of you that loves you more than anything else. The part of you that loves you more than anything else has created roadblocks to lead you to yourself.

You are not going in the right direction unless there is something pricking you in the side, telling you, "Look here! This way!" That part of you loves you so much that it doesn't want you to lose the chance. It will go to extreme measures to wake you up, it will make you suffer greatly if you don't listen.

What else can it do?

That is its purpose."

— **A.H. Almaas.**

Day 22: Reconnecting with your Path of Purpose

Our core values pave our path to purpose. Identifying core values involves reflecting on the most essential principles of our being. Envision an ideal day aligned with your values, noting the key elements that make it fulfilling. Consider community, family, service, honesty, compassion, adventure, integrity, kindness, growth, perseverance, and creativity. Take time to think about what matters most in all aspects of your life.

◣ **Phase 6** Self-Compassion and Connection (Days 22-24)

Day 22 - Write: Reflect on this ideal day. In which moments would you feel a vital purpose or fulfilment? Perhaps it would be serving others, overcoming fears, or making meaningful connections. How would these experiences align with your deepest values? Are there any common themes within these experiences? In which moments of life have you felt most fulfilled or proud? Which values do you associate with those experiences? How do your core values contribute to your sense of purpose? Craft a final statement that reconnects you with your path of purpose, focusing on what illuminates your soul's desires. Your statement could be written as a personal mantra or an affirmation, reinforcing your commitment to meaningful living. An example could be that my purpose is to facilitate understanding, growth and acceptance within others by investigating myself and inspiring development through sharing personal experiences and life lessons.

Day 23: Alignment with purpose

Gautama Buddha spoke on the importance of 'right livelihood' to create a purpose-led living that serves and doesn't harm others. Evaluate your current lifestyle, relationships, pursuits, and activities. Consider how they align with your identified values.

◗ Phase 6 Self-Compassion and Connection (Days 22-24)

Day 23 - Write: Write down your core values. Prioritise them in order of importance. Do your life choices, careers, and relationships align with your purpose and values? Which are deal-breakers? Which are less critical? Use these values to craft a statement defining your life purpose. It should encapsulate the overarching mission or direction you want to move in based on what's most important to you. For example, building on the reference statement from day 22, my life's purpose is to teach others to discover themselves and find joy in their existence. I'll create engaging and valuable therapeutic techniques based on my formal education, experiential learnings and personal healing.

_____

_____

_____

_____

_____

_____

_____

_____

_____

_____

_____

_____

_____

_____

_____

_____

_____

_____

_____

Day 24: Self-Reflection, Authenticity and Attachment

We have been developing the capacity to recognise the presence of authenticity and differentiate between it and our attachments. As we explored earlier, our attachments and personality are adaptations to our authentic being, implemented to reconnect with love or re-establish safety when we perceive it as lost. These adaptations can manifest as a sense of emptiness, longing, or a feeling that something essential is missing. The contemporary spiritual teacher, A.H. Almaas, explores the idea that individuals may carry emotional or psychological gaps within them, which he calls "holes." These holes represent areas of emotional or psychological deficiency, usually stemming from unmet childhood needs, unresolved issues, or other early life experiences. Almaas suggests individuals may develop defence mechanisms or adaptive behaviours to cope with these perceived deficiencies. In the context of self-discovery and personal growth, addressing these "holes" becomes extremely valuable. It's proposed that by exploring and understanding these emotional gaps, individuals can embark on a transformative journey to heal and integrate these aspects of themselves. This process involves deep Self-inquiry, compassion, and a willingness to confront and explore the underlying perceptions associated with these perceived holes.

Day 24 - Write: Which self-beliefs lead you to suppress your authenticity? What 'holes' can you identify that your adaptive behaviours are trying to protect? What fears, judgments or core beliefs may underlie these perceptions? Can you recognise your autonomic responses and reactions when forsaking responsibility? Which societal pressures or external expectations have influenced your expression of authenticity? How have familial, cultural or societal norms shaped your perception of Self? How would you differentiate your authentic Self from your adaptive self, and can you recognise when one has shown up over the other?

_____

_____

_____

_____

_____

_____

_____

_____

_____

_____

_____

_____

_____

_____

_____

_____

_____

Day 25: The Love Letter

Celebrate your progress and commitment by writing yourself a love letter.
A twist on the popular trauma relief exercise of the grief letter, this practice
is an opportunity to acknowledge your efforts, recognising and appreciating
the consistent effort you've dedicated throughout this book. Highlight the
specific achievements and milestones you've reached during this course.
Express gratitude for the commitment, resilience, and growth you've
demonstrated. Be thankful for your Self-kindness and acknowledge the
positive impact of your efforts on your well-being.

◖ Phase 7 Reflections (Days 25-30)

Day 25 - Write: Free-write from your past to your present Self. Use the following prompts to guide you in writing your letter:

Visualisation, joy, and gratitude.
I love it when you...
It made me happy that...
I'm pleased...

Energy, healing and beauty.
It moved me when you...
I feel healed when you...
It invigorates me when...
I'm happy that...

Appreciation, recognition, and responsibility.
I thank you for...
I recognise...
I'm responsible for...

Serenity and reassurance.
I'm calm when you...
It makes me secure that...
I feel held when you...
My inner child feels
safe when...

Intentions, solutions & wishes.
I hope...
I have learned...
My wish is...

What I want from the relationship is.
I love you...
I forgive you...
I appreciate you...

_____

_____

_____

_____

_____

_____

_____

_____

_____

_____

_____

_____

_____

_____

_____

_____

_____

_____

_____

_____

_____

_____

_____

_____

_____

_____

_____

_____

_____

_____

_____

_____

_____

_____

_____

_____

Now, find a mirror in a private space and read your letter back to yourself.

Day 26: Visitation of your Past Self

As we learn to confront and accept the shadow parts of ourselves, meaning those parts we've formed attachments to hide, we begin to feel safer standing in our authenticity. We have started disengaging our subconscious autopilot self. We release our programmed and conditioned approval-seeking parts by trusting our intuition.

Phase 7 Reflections (Days 25-30)

Day 26 - Write: Revisit your first daily entry once more. What do you notice about your Self description this time? Observe and write down any noticeable changes or shifts in your perception of yourself from days one and two. What do you believe is still valid? What has changed on the journey you've undertaken over the past 25 days? Describe how your understanding of identity, authentic behaviours, responsibility, and behaviour patterns has evolved. What recurring themes or patterns can you identify in your old description that you've actively addressed or transformed during this program?

Day 27: Personal Commitments

During today's exercise, consider the key takeaways from your Self-discovery journey. Spotlight the most impactful insights, behavioural shifts, or realisations you've gained during the program that you wish to continue developing.

◖ Phase 7 Reflections (Days 25-30)

Day 27 - Write: Craft a personal mission statement or declaration of commitment to ensure you never fall back into your subconscious autopilot patterns. Outline your intentions for continued growth, emphasising the values and principles you want to embody daily. What commitments will you honour regarding your mental, physical, emotional and spiritual growth? Who are you without your adaptations, attachments and conditioned beliefs? How do you want to spend your remaining years? What do you want to focus on creating? What areas of growth do you want to flourish in? How do you want to show up in the world? If you feel brave, consider sharing your statement with your community for accountability, connection, and support.

Day 28: Cultivating Sustainable Habits

Much of our healing comes from recognising the presence of our authenticity and creating sustainable habits of responsibility. We must learn to form a trustworthy bond with our authentic Self, ensuring it feels heard, encouraged and expressed. Reflect on the habits or practices that you've explored throughout this book. Consider how this awareness has positively impacted your well-being and how you could continue developing consistent, authentic habit patterns.

◣ Phase 7 Reflections (Days 25-30)

Day 28 - Write: How does your authenticity communicate with you? When is it most commonly present? Which habits promote connection within? How could you embrace the lesson of responsibility through authentic acts? What experiences could you implement to sustain your accountability? Which habitual integrations could you practice daily to nurture your personal growth and healing? How would your relationship with yourself and others look if you continued in this direction?

_____

_____

_____

_____

_____

_____

_____

_____

_____

_____

_____

_____

_____

_____

_____

_____

_____

_____

Day 29: Self-Inquiry as a Way of Being

Recognising and building a relationship with our authentic Self requires compassion for all our parts. The protective parts, particularly, require the practice of objective witnessing, meaning compassionately observing and hearing their desires without attaching, acting on, or identifying with them.

Day 29 - Write: How could you bring compassion to the unhealed parts of yourself? When facing internal conflicts, how could you proceed with Self-reflection? Which desires do these parts like to express? What could their intention or motivation be? How could you ensure they feel heard and accepted whilst respecting your authenticity? How do these parts affect your relationships? Reflect on your interactions with others. How could you build and maintain healthier relationships by bringing compassionate awareness to these parts? How could you stay true to your authentic, connective Self as you do this?

_____

_____

_____

_____

_____

_____

_____

_____

_____

_____

_____

_____

_____

_____

_____

_____

_____

_____

Day 30: Community

The final aspect of Self-realisation is community integration and appreciation. Altruistic teachers and guides choose to gift their teachings. Thanks to their dedication to healing familial wounds, changing responses, and learning to hold their pain by understanding and accepting their parts deeply, we, too, can uncover ourselves. When we are offered this knowledge and shown how to apply it through experience, it becomes our wisdom. These few souls have made the world better for many by making themselves better first.

You've now brought awareness to the different parts of yourself and begun embracing them. You show up better for your loved ones and have more valuable interactions with others because you've discovered intimacy within. Having explored the beliefs and perceptions of the protective mind and its parts, we understand the universal truth that we all want to be loved, understood and accepted for who we are. Much of our suffering is due to a false perception of separateness. Recognising we're all connected through this human experience, community becomes paramount. As my teachers bestowed on me and I now share with you, one key aspect of Self-work is a willingness to share our journey to support others in theirs.

◖ Phase 7 Reflections (Days 25-30)

Day 30 - Write: How could you share, support and engage in communal growth? In what ways could you encourage and facilitate societal responsibility through Self-awareness? What would you hope for others to find within? What does an authentic expression of gratitude look like for you? Could you give thanks to those who have supported and guided you personally? Who would you thank? Write a sentence for each person and share it with them. Which of these things would you say to yourself? Can you identify someone or some cause that could benefit from your authentic, loving connection? We have a community set up for Self-work practitioners. If you join, consider sharing your reflections and realisations with the community, and if moved to do so, consider gifting a copy of this book to someone you love, are grateful for, or feel this work could support. Invite others to reflect on their experiences and offer support in navigating their healing. Encourage community discussion by sharing your insights on authenticity and attachment, your developments, and your Self-understanding.

_____

_____

_____

_____

_____

_____

_____

_____

_____

_____

_____

_____

_____

_____

_____

Thank you for your trust.

Your ongoing commitment to Self-discovery plays a unique role in creating a world devoid of unnecessary suffering—no more missed opportunities for love.

www.ingramcontent.com/pod-product-compliance
Lightning Source LLC
Chambersburg PA
CBHW062113080426

42734CB00012B/2845